Of Christmas, Of Winter

Of Christmas, Of Winter

Poems to Warm the Soul

John L. Breska

RESOURCE *Publications* • Eugene, Oregon

OF CHRISTMAS, OF WINTER
Poems to Warm the Soul

Copyright © 2021 John L. Breska. All rights reserved. Except for brief quotations in critical publications or reviews, no part of this book may be reproduced in any manner without prior written permission from the publisher. Write: Permissions, Wipf and Stock Publishers, 199 W. 8th Ave., Suite 3, Eugene, OR 97401.

Resource Publications
An Imprint of Wipf and Stock Publishers
199 W. 8th Ave., Suite 3
Eugene, OR 97401

www.wipfandstock.com

PAPERBACK ISBN: 978-1-6667-1643-6
HARDCOVER ISBN: 978-1-6667-1644-3
EBOOK ISBN: 978-1-6667-1645-0

AUGUST 19, 2021

To God.

To Grace and Walter, my parents, with love.

Contents

Acknowledgements | viii
Introduction | ix

A Christmas Prayer | 1
Winter Birds | 2
A Christmas Prayer for Those I've Known | 3
The Winter World | 4
A Christmas Tale | 5
The Votive Line | 7
A Merry Christmas | 8
The Soldier Tree | 9
A Native American Christmas | 10
The Snow Ballet (a children's dance) | 11
A Nuthatch on Christmas Day | 12
The Sleigh | 14
A Simple Christmas | 16
The Shepherd's Account | 17
Bethlehem City | 18
The Fourth Wise Man | 20
Christmas, Two Thousand Fifteen | 21
The Dawning of New Snow | 22

Christmas Day Greetings | 23

The Christmas Box | 24

Christmas Eve | 25

The Christmas Blues | 26

Christmas Joy | 27

The Choir Boy | 28

Christmas Memories | 29

Snowflakes | 30

Christmas Morning; Eight Years Old | 31

Buck on The Run | 32

Snow | 33

Christmas Observations | 34

Silver Hair | 35

Christmas Spirit | 36

Christmas Thoughts, Nineteen Eighty–Two | 38

One Small Boy and Christmas | 39

Merry Christmas | 40

First Snow and More | 41

Merry Christmas, Two Thousand Eleven | 42

On Christmas Eve | 43

Mississippi Christmas Eve | 44

New York State of Winter | 45

The Homeless Man | 46

Buffalo Hill | 47

Snowbound | 49

BIBLIOGRAPHY | 51

Acknowledgements

It would only be proper to acknowledge the Dominican nuns, as well as lay teachers, and the Catholic Priests of Saint Thomas Aquinas, Milwaukee, who helped lay the foundation, through my grade school years.

A sincere thank you goes out to my dear wife, Deborah, for her contribution of the watercolor art for the cover.

Introduction

I HAVE COMPILED A group of poems which fall into that season we call winter. Christians celebrate Christmas or the birth of our Lord during the winter season so, I have mixed Christmas related poems with winter related poetry that I've written over the past forty years. My goal is to have the poetry warm you through these chilling days.

A Christmas Prayer

When all the snowflakes settle down
across the north and my hometown,
when *Silent Night*[1] is sung again
and joy replaces all the pain

Tis then that I will say a prayer
in hope, that it will ride on air,
that peace will enter every heart,
a seed, hard planted from the start

For what is life without a song
but misery that stays too long,
a flower that will never bloom
expresses not and fades too soon

May joy be written on each face,
may we be touched by God's own grace,
may we be given eyes to see,
the road to true prosperity

Let's put to rest, the book of hate,
in love, may we all congregate
and in my stocking place these things,
the attributes that kindness brings

---

1. Gruber and Mohr, Silent Night, Title

Winter Birds

The mourning dove sits quietly at bay,
gray feather's ruffled to the wind,
it waits for some small change upon the day
but snow falls harder to no end

A nuthatch lands upon the feeder's edge,
in search of some small tasty seed,
she looks at me as if to make a pledge
of thanks, that I've fulfilled her need

The memory of cardinals pass by,
a color bright against the snow,
a ruby on an alabaster sky,
a holly berry red, you know

The suet swings in winter rhythm time,
a small woodpecker makes his play
and from my point of window's view, I rhyme
with birds that come and go their way

A Christmas Prayer for Those I've Known

We lose some friends along the way
but quiet time on Christmas Day,
I find a corner and I pray
that life has blessed those I have known
and they have found their way back home,
to heaven's gate, should they have passed
or found a trail far from mine,
which took them to their destinies
alone, or with their families

I pray all's well in God's own time,
I hope they're blessed and doing fine
beyond December's thoughtful days,
through life and how life often plays,
with paths we never dreamt we'd blaze

the lessons learned are gifts of worth
to all who've shared this troubled earth

The Winter World

I'm inspired by the frost upon the glass
and the winter world that's surely come to pass,
I am patiently awaiting the arrival of the snow,
for it brings back winter memories, you know

Like the times I used to skate down by the pond
or walk within the woods that lie beyond,
catching snowflakes on my mittens so I'd see the different shapes
and the pine boughs that hung down like clumps of grapes

Ran my sled down mighty hills between the trees,
recollecting that I did it with much ease,
often shoveled snow for profit, as we went from home to home,
like the nomads of the north, us kids would roam

Well, the best of friends will surely disagree
and I'm sure it's happened to both you and me,
now, the way that we would solve it in an understanding light,
is to simply have a massive snowball fight

There were icicles that hung from every house
and the ever, tiny footprints of a mouse,
as he looked for warmer quarters on a cold December day,
soon, the sun would melt the evidence away

Now my cobweb covered shovel holds my eye,
as I look up toward the heavens at the sky,
I see water crystallizing as it falls, for goodness sakes,
the arrival of the season's first snowflakes

A Christmas Tale

Adventures come in varied lengths and size
while times appear when children must be wise,
a given task brings joy when it's complete
and so, I closed the door then reached the street

Five single dollar bills from dear old dad,
a challenge and the task were what I had,
the city sidewalk loomed in front of me
as I went hunting for a Christmas tree

Black, rubber boots with metal clips undone
were on my feet and chimed when I would run,
the snow banks were at least at shoulder height,
as this young lad of twelve strolled through the night

The corner came and went as left, I turned
my nose caught smoke from chimneys as wood burned,
the colored lights in storefronts blinked in time,
a snowball went from hand to a Stop Sign

The tree lot was alive with customers,
I weaved my way around the boughs with fears
and hoped my choice would please both mom and dad;
so many trees; one choice was all I had

A wrinkled brow brought me to eye my fir,
I paid the man while wishing Christmas cheer,
tied rope near trunk then slowly pulled away,
anticipating what the folks would say

I reached our porch then got dad's helping hand
as he went on to tackle the tree stand,
quite soon the tree stood in our living room,
with lights, bright ornaments, and tinsel strewn

Like presents wrapped, those days are boxed in me,
sweet memories beneath my Christmas tree,
they're opened when December finds its way
and brings that joy I found one winter day

The Votive Line

Reflections of a midnight sky on one, cold, Christmas Eve,
the stars shine down upon a man who cannot stay nor leave,
his destiny is passing through this period of time,
no king nor shepherd is his claim, but just a man in line

A periodic snowflake falls upon those standing fast,
they set upon the middleman who is not first or last,
his lips move silently in prayer, warm breath against the cold,
he is not measured by his age; he is not young or old

An hour passes by in life and soon he's at the door,
one hundred steps past rows of pews, perhaps one less, one more,
another twenty minutes, there are just two souls ahead,
soft organ music fills the air to where they all are led

The man approaches slowly, as his eyes take in the sight,
he kneels down in reverence, for holy is this night,
a tear forms as he lights his candle for the memory,
of one small child born to save the world and set men free

A Merry Christmas

Christmas is the time of peace,
let us all renew our lease
and try to rise above ourselves,
like all good children and fine elves

See their faces all aglow,
full of love, for all should know,
there's hope and faith to go around,
this gift of heart, inside, is found

Its cost, a kindness to a soul,
without another hidden goal,
without us getting anything,
will get the angels all to sing

A good deed opens up the door
and feeling good we do much more,
come decorate the inner man,
while time allows us that we can

A Merry Christmas, as we go,
our praises to the King we know,
one star, that all should find their way,
on this coming Christmas day

The Soldier Tree

Through timeless battles on this world,
a soldier's loss has grieved the heart
of mother dearest, who gave birth
and then all others who in part

Had known the woman or the man,
who gave their lives for their belief
but there we find the emptiness,
the hole which we fill with our grief

And so, when Christmas time is nigh
and evergreens are jeweled, once plain,
there is another tree, I've heard
that's decorated with each name

Great images of soldiering,
where silence is the song, they sing;
the soldier tree of fallen men,
where boughs hang heavy, for they bring

Remembrance of great sacrifice,
where campaign metals can't suffice,
the loss of those who once we knew,
who hang upon the spruce of blue

A Native American Christmas

The scene is an Indian's camp near a river,
a child is waiting, he's starting to shiver,
his father is hunting for what could be dinner
as snow starts to quietly fall

The young boy adds wood as he stokes up the fire,
soon, evening approaches, he's starting to tire,
he prays to the spirits, who live a bit higher
that father comes home without stall

The hour is late and his mother is troubled,
she steps from the tepee, her words slightly muddled,
the snow deepens quickly, soon, they are both huddled
around the warm fire but small

The sound of the lone wolf cries on through the flurry,
the mother and son exchange glances of worry,
and both hope within, that their man would please hurry
then suddenly they hear him call

He rides into camp with a deer and two pheasants,
some birch for the fire to give it some essence,
and brings them a fox and a mink skin for presents,
this Indian brave, returns tall

This picture is painted some time, late December,
a Christmas, three Cherokee's fondly remember,
they woke the next morning near fire's low ember,
a family still, after all

The Snow Ballet (a children's dance)

Picture a morning so silent and bright,
outside the window the world has turned white,
somewhere an orchestra tunes for the score,
carefully, children slip out the back door

Fuzzy wool hats cover young, little heads,
multiple colors in greens, blues and reds,
snow pants and jackets, bright mittens are worn,
snowflakes are falling, a snowman is born

Start of a season, for winter is here,
Christmas and Santa, and flying reindeer,
don't forget God and good will toward all men
or we might never see snowflakes again

Young boys and girls in a world of their own,
dance over snowdrifts and right past their home,
over and under those ivory stars,
too small to shovel or brush off the cars

Snow in the boots, rosy cheeks, such a sight
all through the day and then, part of the night,
building great snow forts where once there were lawns,
then to their beds with a face full of yawns

A Nuthatch on Christmas Day

I stood beside an evergreen as snow fell all around,
a tender silence filled my ears; a northern winter sound,
a nuthatch landed on a bough and eyed me through and through,
we both, explorers on this day, in search of something new

The nuthatch flew on branches high, to see what was to see,
while I walked up an empty hill to find tranquility,
the wind blew snow in gusts and swirls, while I stood fast
in place,
my beard and eyebrows frosted white against a rosy face

I shouted out a strong, "hello" much muted by the storm,
I thought of people in their homes near hearths, to keep
them warm,
remembered those unfortunates, who had no place to go,
who lived their days and long, long nights in places most
don't know

This Christmas morning gave new sight to goodwill and to peace,
renewing all I once believed; extension of my lease,
the nuthatch landed once again amongst the winter wood,
she brought along a friend or two and then I understood

It's good to find a quiet place and talk to God alone
but man needs to return to man and share the spirit's tone,
I came down from the hill that day awakened to my life,
a lighter heart, a warmer soul, a man now void of strife

Returning to my little town, I hailed the souls who passed,
I felt to be a part of them, no longer an outcast,
I looked toward church then doubled back and entered on this day,
I joined in prayer with all these souls, that God would guide our way

And now some long years later when I walk the wooded trail,
the nuthatch joins me as a comfort and we both do hail,
all God's creatures large and small who know the reason why,
a star once shone 'or Bethlehem; a sign high in the sky

The Sleigh

Shoveled the snowdrifts as a lad
but never a time so down and sad,
than finding Santa's sleigh one night,
beneath a bent and dark streetlight

No reindeer 'round that I could see,
just Santa, lying 'neath a tree,
no Christmas blessings for mankind,
instead, one empty sled; my find

Rested my laurels deep in white,
while asking God about this plight,
soon angels gathered, one and all,
and sang a sweet but chilling call

Told, in the storm, an accident,
where on to heaven Santa went,
his mission in great disarray,
when Santa simply lost his way

Remained, a button and black glove,
one finger pointing straight above,
all hearts would weep to hear such news,
thought I, who found these many clues

So, left to my own destiny
I donned the suit so I might see,
if there was goodness on this Earth
and some remembered our Lord's birth

Found souls of love all warm and bright,
a tender world beneath starlight,
for most, there was great hope for peace,
bag full of faith gave me new lease

And so, it was on Christmas Eve,
I took the reins and gave reprieve,
a dream but truly wide awake,
by filling in, for goodness sake

A Simple Christmas

The gift of giving comes to mind,
each present, of a special kind,
when times are economic tough
and we can't give a bunch of stuff

Our choices find reality,
instead of promos on TV,
a thoughtful offering from heart,
which blossoms gratitude in part

An apple or a cherry pie,
brings satisfaction with a sigh,
a wreath, with holly and pine cone,
will greet the entrance of a home

A knitted scarf and hat will warm,
more than a head in winter storm,
hot, homemade cider fills the air;
a treasured drink that all can share

A Christmas card made personal,
the art and words from one's own soul,
a gentleness, that all will find,
a prayer for peace, for all mankind

The Shepherd's Account

I was a shepherd on a hill,
tending my flock in the cold, blue night,
watching for hungry wolves and all,
keeping my sheep within my sight

Clear were the heavens, grand, the thrill,
following star as it came to light,
over a manger, very small,
shining down beams so very bright

Something within began to fill;
love took the place where there once was fright,
I blew the horn, the shepherd's call
and we saw Him, all bathed in white

Bethlehem City

A night much like that sacred night when He was born
in manger,
came once again on city streets corrupt, with filth and danger,
this time, a woman and a man who had but half of nothing,
tried urgently to find a place, for winter wasn't bluffing

Rejections followed every knock, while some doors had
no answer,
this one, expecting, treated like a leper or a cancer,
the couple found an alley with a recess as protection,
some garbage cans to slow the wind, with cardboard intervention

She settled down, he watched the watch, and comforted his Mary,
a single roof light shone on them, which made both a bit wary,
a world of drugs and crime plus death, was never known
as subtle,
for nothing good came from this place, there was no
street rebuttal

The time had come, she came to birth; a new babe in December,
her Joe talked gently, telling her, this day they would remember,
four rappers sauntered down the alley and surprised the couple,
they all looked on with wonder, singing peace, to each
man's trouble

Three found their way to where the boy lay in an orange crate,
voicing,
"We're homeless, women and one man, and heard the song,
rejoicing!
This is an offspring of the God who guides us through tomorrow,
we bring three gifts of hope and faith and joy to replace sorrow"

This baby smiling broadly, in the midst of sewers and gutters
gave way to realizing that we all are bound as brothers,
He cooed, for life was fresh and new, dawn's greeting, bringing
first light
and something new was felt that morn as fear left with that
dark night

The Fourth Wise Man

There came to pass one night so clear,
a star, which drew good hearts and souls
toward understanding peace on earth,
to deep inside each man's own worth,
the "Way" as in one child's birth,
God's nurturing of all man's goals

There also came a stranger near,
a man, drawn onward by the light,
all needs were second to the first,
the quenching of an endless thirst,
to reach its source before he burst,
and rest his eyes upon this sight

There was the break of morning's tear;
the dew and mist that comes with dawn,
the man drew nigh yet no soul shone,
the stable sat there all alone,
for all had journeyed back to home,
except one angel deep in song

"There is a melody to hear,
that in this manger some time past
the birth of goodness truly came,
dear man, the truth in hearts remain,
to give us peace and ease our pain,
new life upon the waters cast"

Christmas, Two Thousand Fifteen

Soon the color paper flies
around the room as children's eyes
grow large at what their vision sees,
while grownups hope the choices, please

Church and sermon, choir sings,
the gift of love is what God brings,
then back to home where dinner waits,
as family participates

A schnapps to settle food to rest
as kids give parents one last test,
tired eyelids close the day,
and Christmas slowly fades away

We look to New Year's in a week
and hope the next year is less bleak,
we dread the bills that will arrive
but thank God we are still alive

A long, deep sigh before our head
is carried off to waiting bed,
and so, goes Christianity,
Santa folklore, and pine tree

One hopes the message of God's grace
stays within that inner place,
where free will struggles each new day,
as each soul, finds its own way

The Dawning of New Snow

New sunrise brought the magic to my eyes
and cloaked in winter wonderment, the earth was void of lies,
for everything was crystallized in vivid shades of white
and I was briefly blinded by the light

There was not one impression in the snow,
for nothing that did live or breathe, had yet, been on the go
and all the world was radiant while I was left in awe,
immaculate, the vision that I saw

Then faintly, I heard thunder in the air,
was this perhaps the end of life, was God filled with despair,
the fear that filled my body, brings a chuckle to me now,
for it was just a dump truck with a plow

Christmas Day Greetings

No greater gift beneath my tree
than love of life and family,
the bows and colored paper, fine,
but souls I know fill up my time,
the holidays light up the eyes
like northern lights in winter skies,
so, make my gifts life's attributes,
for man bares much from his good roots
and let God's love shine through and through,
this Christmas Day for you and you!

The Christmas Box

I wrap an empty box at Christmas
to place beneath the tree,
I put a label on the lid
From: "those who can't gift me"

And when it's time to open presents
I open that one first,
reminding, there are many poor
and them who have it worse

I think of those who won't be gifting
and feel their emptiness,
whose only joy might be the thought;
"today's a smaller mess"

I cannot fix the world we live in
strictly on my own
but I can share my thoughts with you,
within this simple poem

I'll seek a soul who might be weary
and gift them in some way,
this fills my empty box, my friends,
and brightens Christmas Day

Christmas Eve

Carol on the winter wind
moves across December's night,
through the leafless trees, now thinned,
over snow, beneath moonlight

And the voices sing of birth,
for the Christ child has been born,
joy abides upon the earth,
there is calm, where once a storm

Peace comes to the lonely soul,
there is hope for all mankind,
see the star which marks man's goal,
light the way for all to find

The Christmas Blues

I gathered many angel tears from places where they cried,
from sad events like broken homes and when a loved one died,
I put them in a special place where only I would know,
till one such Christmas came to pass, when I was down and low

I found a blue spruce in a lot that seemed to be alone,
and after just a moment's thought, I dragged the poor tree home,
placed it in my wrought iron stand and watered it that day,
I wrapped it in some small blue lights, a very special way

Blue garland and blue ornaments touched every single bough,
a vision of my own blue heart, at least right here and now,
we shared our Christmas Eve as friends, this tree of blue and I,
and times that night we took our turns emitting each a sigh

I thought of all those angel tears and brought them out to see,
if they were still all sad and blue, like me and my blue tree
but they had turned to tiny stars that sparkled oh, so bright,
they brought a joy to my sad face, on this lone, silent night

I carried them outside and tossed them way up in the air,
to light the way for peace and love, so all would be aware
and they turned into angels who all sang of God's sweet grace
and I was born anew, without, the blues upon my face

Christmas Joy

I walk a road called Christmas Time
it lives inside my memories
smiles, presents, lights and essence,
brightly colored Christmas trees,
mangers filled with figurines,
one small lad with many dreams,
shopping for the perfect gift
through a maze of snowy streets,
automated window scenes
in department stores,
people happy, filled with joy,
or so it seemed to this young boy

I often wonder of the fade
as January days rolled by,
as I watch people's sad parade,
as the sparkle leaves their eye,
I guess the greatest gift we have
is love for all, through God, I sigh
and wish we kept His joy, so dear
throughout December and all year

The Choir Boy

All alone on Christmas Eve
I walked the empty streets,
while people were with family,
exchanging gifts and treats

Through the flakes of fallen snow
I heard a precious song,
presented by one choir boy,
who sang both clear and strong

He stood upon a wooden box,
his eyes were on the sky,
he sang of peace, he sang of love,
he sang to God on high

And I saw angels smile on him,
as he voiced out each word,
new feelings moved me from within,
God knows I truly heard!

This message in all innocence,
a song of life and worth,
that graced me on that Christmas Eve
and brought my knees to earth

I'm older now and warmed inside,
my heart is filled with joy,
for life and Christmas mean more now,
Lord! Bless that choir boy

Christmas Memories

As the snowflakes touch my face
there's a peace that settles me,
I remember long ago,
Christmas wrapped in family

Many seasons have gone by
lives have gone their separate ways,
old traditions; memories,
how I miss those yesterdays

Snowflakes

Snowflakes dancing all around,
between the heavens and the ground,
they never make a single sound,
as I move through their space

Little sculptured flakes of white,
sparkle in the evening light,
fall from somewhere out of sight,
upon this small boy's face

As the wind groans soft and sighs,
landscapes change before my eyes,
sent to us from winter skies,
they cover every place

Soft and dainty, one by one,
scooped and shoveled by the ton,
disappears, when comes the sun,
at quite a rapid pace

Christmas Morning; Eight Years Old

Blinked wide upon a pillow in anticipated motion,
awaiting dawn's arrival for a Christmas morning's notion,
bright bows and colored paper might hide something for this thinker,
behaved throughout the year with manners gentle for a stinker

Quick doze, awake first light, I moved toward evergreen and trimmings,
with hope as my companion, praying hard for no misgivings,
an image bounds across the room as light as angel feathers,
a glimpse, a shadow, between peeks, caught red and white, and leathers

My eyes protruding at the sight of boxes dressed in color,
great curiosity abounds as my mind stretches taller,
the tinsel sways as I move 'round the ornamented branches,
a mental count of presents gives assessment to my chances

Reflecting on past days ago when from his lap I'd spoken,
of what exactly was my heart's desire as a token,
I asked for something special, for the meaning of the season,
not just a bauble that would sit, one day, past rhyme and reason

But now the time arrived and dreams had reached my state of being,
the ribbons and the paper torn away allowed me seeing,
that deep inside the treasured box was more than things that please us,
three kings, the shepherds, Mary, Joseph and a baby Jesus

Buck on The Run

I came to the shore of a winter pond
and pondered a deer on the shore beyond,
I thought of the days when the hunt came first,
the folly, now knowing I'd lost the thirst

I tended my thoughts of more recent times
and gazed at the buck through the northern pines,
the wind shifted then and he raised his head,
a glance back at me and away he fled

Reflections of life, now and long ago,
trails well hid under fallen snow,
so quickly the deer slips behind the bough,
as if he once was but is not there now

Was I the man on that given day
or the buck that had run just to get away,
far from the hunt over rock and stream,
deep into nature, where all men dream

Snow

As the sun on morning breaks,
much the sound an angel makes,
just before the wind song wakes,
so, begins the snow

When each autumn passes by
and the geese have cleared the sky,
somewhere in the clouds on high,
comes first winter's snow

White as feathers from a dove,
water chilled and spun above,
soft and peaceful as true love,
come pure flakes of snow

Man cannot quite duplicate
that which moves through nature's gate,
loved by some, yet other's hate,
still, it comes, the snow

Christmas Observations

My spirit rises with the season
and I'd like to think the greatest reason
is, I'm reminded of the Christ child
born so very meek and mild,
in conditions less than pleasant
not as royalty but peasant,
stabled with both fowl and beast,
shepherds; soon, men from the east

All of this I find brings hope,
to a world that cannot cope
with being human all year long,
it's sad we only sing God's song
at certain times through the year,
if I were God, I'd shed a tear,
for mankind's troubled with a hate
that seems to only permeate

As I grow older, I pray, see
where all men will find unity,
an understanding of God's way,
not just at Christmas but each day

Silver Hair

She's alone on Christmas Eve,
much too old to decorate,
though, in God does she believe
her faith's shaken on this date

She is sewing in her chair,
thinking much on yesterdays,
years before her silver hair,
times that thrived on home cooked ways

Tired eyes look to a frame
on the table next to her,
it's a picture of her flame,
passed beyond, this time last year

Humming *Silent Night*[2] real low,
one great tear forms from her eye,
in her prayers, she prays to go,
"for dear Lord, alone am I"

Through the window of her heart
winter sends a colder tone,
solitaire takes no one's part,
living in an old age home

2. Gruber and Mohr, *Silent Night*, Title

Christmas Spirit

Ornament box was dusted off
but not without a sneeze and cough,
then brought down from its resting place
by dear, old Dad, with smudge on face

Countless amounts of colored lights
to warm those cold December nights,
to dazzle all the neighbor's eyes
and pilots over friendly skies

Cast iron tree stand; green and red
was found beneath my sister's bed,
with last year's candy cane inside
and some poor cricket that had died

Bright strands of lights adorned the tree,
laced gently by the family,
the smell of pine throughout our home,
began to set the Christmas tone

Sang about Santa all day long,
when evening came, we changed our song
to *Silent Night*[3], with reverence,
for all of us, it made good sense

Touched on those days that might have been
so long ago, I know not when,
in someone's house, on someone's street
across the years of snow and sleet

3. Gruber and Mohr, *Silent Night*, Title

Creating *Christmas Spirit* takes
a healing of each year's heartaches,
and love, like tinsel on the tree
shines forth from you and even me

Christmas Thoughts, Nineteen Eighty-Two

I stood outside on the day of Christmas
and wondered how many knew,
that the spirit of God touched a young and pure virgin
and the Son of our God slowly grew

As snow fell down on my face that moment,
I thought of the poor, lonely souls,
who wandered through life, always caught up in dying,
always walking a path of hot coals

Remembered to what this time did honor,
the Son of our God had been born,
a gift from the Almighty One to us all,
to make whole the broken and torn

Life to all who would ask for forgiveness,
God only wanted to please us,
to show us His love, which we lost throughout time,
he gave us this morn, baby Jesus

One Small Boy and Christmas

This is the story of one small boy
who never knew of a single toy,
before each Christmas he would pray,
that Santa would bless him in this way

It didn't have to be something grand
his only need, that it filled his hand,
"Some simple token," he cried out loud,
"would make this little one very proud"

Soon, Christmas Eve was upon this lad,
always a good boy and seldom bad,
patiently waiting for a sign,
would Santa Claus really come this time

Way after midnight when small boys sleep
Santa stopped quickly without a peep,
and placed in his hand from afar,
a piece of our Lord's very own star

Waking, the lad was consumed with joy
for what he received did surpass a toy,
an understanding of this day
and how a small child had come man's way

Yes, giving way to a warmer light
and putting peace back into man's night,
off in the distance sleigh bells rang,
"Oh! Peace be to all," the snow elf sang

Merry Christmas

Christmas is the time of peace,
let us all renew our lease
and try to rise above ourselves,
like all good children and fine elves

Little faces all aglow,
full of love, for all should know,
there's hope and faith to go around,
the gift of heart, inside, is found

Its cost, a kindness to a soul,
without another hidden goal,
without us getting anything,
will get the angels all to sing

A good deed gives way to the door
and feeling good, we do much more,
come decorate the inner man,
while time allows us that we can

A Merry Christmas as we go,
our praises to the King we know,
one star, that all should find their way,
on this, the coming Christmas Day

First Snow and More

A canvas transformation from a bleak November brown,
among the darkened hours that I sleep in my hometown
and when my eyes regain their sight,
an altered state has touched the night,
has covered all the browns with white,
for snow has fallen down

My feelings have been altered by the change that's taken place,
a look of child's wonderment has replaced a grimmer face,
the thoughts of sledding down a hill,
and snowball fights give me a thrill,
but then, the shovel waits there, still,
to which there is no race

Yet, for the moment, drifting snow has warmed my
seasoned heart
and even though there's work to do, it is a work of art,
for when the sculpting of it's done
and snowmen wave to everyone,
the shovel down and comes the sun,
a new snow will soon start

Merry Christmas, Two Thousand Eleven

Born a Christian by tradition,
it is my path; our way
it's what I've known to give me peace
and guide me to my God,
as so, it is with each man's faith
which comforts him at night,
no harm in being different
as long as God's in sight,
so, as we celebrate our day
we send peace on, another way,
for all ways are the same,
if love abides in each man's heart,
for what is man without his Lord
but restless, wrought and bored,
still, given guidance love does fruit
and we, as souls, are in accord

On Christmas Eve

If I were an angel on Christmas Eve
I'd carry my faith, here, upon my sleeve,
I'd sing of the coming of peace on earth,
I'd harmonize sweet, of a single birth

If I were an angel on Christmas Eve
I'd voice out my praises; in song I'd weave,
I'd stand by the shepherds and flocks in awe,
I'd rise on the joy of the things I saw

If I were an angel on Christmas Eve
I'd bury my sadness and cease to grieve,
I'd stand beside wise men and know my heart,
I'd understand we each, all have our part

If I were an angel on Christmas Eve
I'd find this a miracle to believe,
I'd look on with ass and the oxen too,
I'd watch with the doves as new hope came true

If I were an angel on Christmas Eve
I'd glow for the fabric that God does weave,
I'd tender my thoughts in the coming days,
If I were an angel, I'd change my ways

Mississippi Christmas Eve

No snow in Mississippi on this December's Eve
but cold, still, air, makes me aware and faith adorns my sleeve,
I was raised a Christian boy, a Midwest worker's son,
we churched on Sundays, prayed all week, and prayed
when day was done

I drifted through religions throughout my grownup years
and found them all to be a place to rest a person's fears,
God has always cared for me regardless what His name
and as I understand it years ago, his Son, He came

He tried to give us guidance but our hearts all went astray,
He died and said He'd come again to guide us on our way,
He never taught to anger or kill another soul,
His only thought, salvation, being that the only goal

The stars all glisten brightly on this blessed Christmas morn,
while calm replaces chaos in this world where I was born,
if only for this moment we can shelf our foolish pride,
let's pray for God's sweet blessing for He is our only guide

New York State of Winter

Quiet snowflakes start to fall,
autumn's over, after all,
winter's come to old New York,
I smell the cool, crisp air

Fireplaces filled with oak,
chimneys showing streams of smoke,
scarves and mittens, hats, and boots,
good children please prepare

North of Saratoga Springs,
I hear *Jack Frost* proudly sings,
through the aspen and the pine,
new travelers, take care

People heading north to ski,
some, content to watch TV,
others skating on a pond,
alone or in a pair

Soon the ornaments and lights,
soon those ever, silent nights,
boys and girls all full of dreams,
please Santa, be aware

The Homeless Man

Not good to be the homeless man when Christmas comes to town,
he tries real hard to have good cheer and hides away that frown
but winters in the north are harsh, quite grueling to stay warm,
the days are managed better, for there's shelter from the storm

But when the stores close down at night true warmth evades the flock
and bundled up like Eskimos they watch each evening's clock,
some factories that run all night but laws prevent him there,
the heat goes out the chimney while those homeless, often stare

The shelters too are limited, they're short on many beds,
the soup's already watered down to feed those hungry heads,
you say, "go out and find a job," but some have issues too,
they're coming from a different place that works for me and you

Yes, Christmas will have come and gone as winter does arrive
and many weeks with frigid temps will test, to stay alive,
so, keep in mind the down and out, as winter days go by
and lend a hand now, if you can, know, but for God go I

Buffalo Hill

The snow was whiting out the day as we climbed the hill again,
great steam rose from their snouts like smoke and their eyes
shone from their pen,
they watched the colored outfits rise then slide back down
the hill,
on saucers, stomachs, sleds and skis to catch that winter thrill

Kids gathered from around our town where zoo gave way to park,
where the elms and oaks looked down upon the bison, large
and dark,
where elevation was the best across our city wide,
where shouts and smiling faces laughed on down the frozen slide

I saw my friends approaching with toboggan right behind,
they brought a candle, waxed the boards; tobogganing refined,
we took our places in a row then forward over crest,
we moved out slow but gained quick speed, much faster than
the rest

I shouted, "tree," we leaned hard right, as we missed the old
jack pine,
one kid fell off his sled far left but he seemed to be just fine,
we slipped between two older oaks as snow turned into ice,
our speed increased another Mach and Patrick shouted, "nice!"

The end was near, we saw the street, and we dropped our feet
to brace
I shed a boot, we spun around, ice and snow flew in my face,
Mike belly flopped, he lost his gloves then slid ten feet away,
looking up he eyed the buffalo, who continued chewing hay

We laughed out loud as we got our gear then we headed to the top,
for we knew we had all afternoon until we had to stop,
well, some fifty years have passed on by and the bison are all gone
but the hill remains a memory in this old man's winter song

Snowbound

The candle melts away as time continues on its journey,
the wax runs down the shaft as sand runs through the hourglass,
I look beyond the window and the geese are moving early,
the snows will all but close the valley pass

And I will sit alone to stoke the fire of contentment,
I'll vision love's soft smile, as she once laid eyes on me,
the sleep shall be a blessing while my thoughts are more
than pleasant
and winter will have brought tranquility

On quiet afternoons I'll write a sonnet for the owl,
I'll paint a portrait of the wind, when it has gone to rest,
upon a ledge, I'll stand and listen to the lone wolf's howl,
then back to shelter, for at night it's best

The solitude has given way to understand just living
and in the quietness, I've found a friend among these bones,
I've watched the natural scope of life in which all things
are giving,
such wisdom then, is right to set the tone

One early morning light will whisper softly through the curtain,
new season sun; the snow melts fast and streams begin to flow,
spring has come a-calling as a friend, of this I'm certain
and I'll be moving on real soon, you know

Bibliography

Gruber, F.X. and Mohr, J. *Silent Night*: Christmas Carol, 1818

www.ingramcontent.com/pod-product-compliance
Lightning Source LLC
Chambersburg PA
CBHW060430050426
42449CB00009B/2219

www.ingramcontent.com/pod-product-compliance
Lightning Source LLC
Chambersburg PA
CBHW060429050426
42449CB00009B/2212